My Thieves

ETHAN PAQUIN is the author of three books of poetry: *The Violence* (Ahsahta Press, 2005); *Accumulus* (Salt, 2003); and *The Makeshift* (UK: Stride, 2002). A native of New Hampshire, he lives and teaches in Buffalo, NY.

Also by Ethan Paquin

The Violence (Ahsahta Press, 2005)
Accumulus (Salt, 2003)
The Makeshift (UK: Stride, 2002)

My Thieves

Ethan Paquin

SALT

Cambridge

PUBLISHED BY SALT PUBLISHING
PO Box 937, Great Wilbraham, Cambridge PDO CB1 5JX United Kingdom

© Ethan Paquin, 2007

The right of Ethan Paquin to be identified as the
author of this work has been asserted by him in accordance
with Section 77 of the Copyright, Designs and Patents Act 1988.

First published 2007

Printed and bound in the United Kingdom by Lightning Source

Typeset in Swift 9.5 / 13

ISBN 978 1 84471 323 3 paperback

Salt Publishing Ltd gratefully acknowledges
the financial assistance of Arts Council England

1 3 5 7 9 8 6 4 2

Contents

DARK TRACTS

Acknowledgements

My gratitude to Graham Foust, Matt Hart, Thomas Heise, Brian Henry, and Theodore Pelton. They took time out of their lives to read the manuscript and comment on it.

Sections of this book have appeared, sometimes in different forms, in the following journals:

The Cincinnati Review: "Brother"
The Colorado Review: "Beautiful Nighttime Churches," "Tigers"
Forklift, Ohio: "[we start with who . . .]", "[dogs are in the mirror . . .]"
Incliner: "I Found the Reason for the Tree"
New American Writing: "Axis of Minimal," "Grandmother Poem," "Toward a Shoreline"
Parthenon West Review: "Stills"
Sentence: "Towers of Buffalo"
Verse: "Hampton"

In online journals:
Cordite: "Asteral"
H_NGM_N: from "[Oratio persona.—]", "[I don't think you see the challenge in the paint]", "[[there is only me here]]", "[man his worries]", "[I need somewhere to begin]", "[perhaps, like the message you scrawled out and tacked near yr desk —]"
Jacket: "Scathologue," "Why Do I Wait for the Thunder Nightly"
Kulture Vulture: "Dream," "Processes (Overheardings)"

"You Just Keep Going (Tong'len #1)" appeared in *PP/FF: An Anthology* (NY: Starcherone Books, 2006), edited by Peter Conners.

My Thieves

My Thieves

I.

My thieves are letters and words
that like wheelbarrows
cart bits of me off and then, FLIP!,
and over an edge—like into a sea,

something like that.

I do the dumping on my own,
the pushing the wheelbarrow,

the sanctioning the carting

the colouring the sea seaish colours

the caring about the sea at all!

Spanning the edge with a thread in dark spare-times
to measure the guts of the thing,

across the belly of the globe thrice and then to Jupiter
the length of a brain decrumpled

and: the colour of the brain darker as the words seep in

II.

I debated an epigraph, perhaps one in Greek,
Greece from which I descend, via my mother, *mater*,
perhaps one in French, France from which I descend,
via *mon pere*,   perhaps even one in Finnish, or even . . .

a subterfuged language . . .

nautical in its ways, looking like cord when transcribed.

I decided against the epigraph. Too much language,
violent

thieving me

Whoest am I

No question for God; a question
        for the human urge to speak,
and whatever compellor it is
        driving the
spoken

ah, wheels

would that the world fleest its riper years   then
all this loudesse to vanish and I to ponder . . .
issues of sleepe
in a silenter time

III.

Oratio persona.—

    make mine not a glutton for language
make mine not an eaten by language
make mine sav'ed though eaten by language
make mine through childrens' eyes saved
make mine though a glutton for language
a teacher of moderation of language
—*a liar, I am madeth, and clearly!*—

make mine image
            "subdued"
as in "the last wine
                has settled"
    as in when in "when in Le Havre . . . when we
stared at sunset   undunning its brick"

issue me not via symbol
via typographical flourish
via the gimmick of the flaneur
via expletive via the use of *cunt*

issue me as clean nighttime sky,
            who[m]ever I addresseth,

issue me sleepe in a silenter time
issue me poesie borne of a silenter time

The poetry is not a silent animal, nor machine

The poetry is a loudness — no veins in shale
but granite, yes, as there are notes in a symphony
but in one observing himself dreaming, none

but in one observing his wife sleeping, none

IV.

I don't think you see the challenge in the paint
you have chosen with which to fund and fuse

    this thing I wanted never to be called Ethan Paquin

Do you mean to speak to me?

I don't think there are paints existeth
for your hopeless goals —

to choose a life of language,   O welcome deafness

O welcome dissolution   Such is elementary,
suchwith each sentence new digested
out shat some original sentence,

instilled I did for purpose in thee,

shunned in pursuit of knowledge and pleasure
by your awful hand, cleave the cock and ink

in pursuit of knowledge and pleasure, dis-
solve mine original riddle and wonder,

solid-born Man, rotted and hacked and thieved

    by words, solidity   the granite   ax'ed,

so many sullying words to fill a sullied vessel
borne of my love borne in my image

Do you mean to speak to me?

As you wield words Do you not sully me?

Do you proffer an escape for me   my dear

my. . .

There are only lakes, and all around
me. . .

V.

[there is only me here]

[of course this text is sui generis:

]

ssh . . . a man alone talks to God

Rarity!

Man in community with pigeons
with God's tongue between each's beak.

VI.

we start with who
then we add [somewhere] end unclear
then we add [somewhere] as
then we add [somewhere] God, oracles?
then we add [somewhere] be a brand
then we add [somewhere] understanding that does
then we add [somewhere] of awareness
then we add [somewhere] unclear then must
then we add [somewhere] are the poem
then we add [somewhere] why then must a not
then we add [somewhere] end. there
then we add [somewhere] an
then we add [somewhere] in means toward
then we add [somewhere] better term? toward
then we add [somewhere] itself. a
then we add [somewhere] is a better
then we add [somewhere] who language as an
then we add [somewhere] an unclear end.
then we add [somewhere] venue for a false
then we add [somewhere] the poet, or innovative
then we add [somewhere] false awareness that does
then we add [somewhere] loves end in
then we add [somewhere] there not; why
then we add [somewhere] the poem be
then we add [somewhere] poet, for lack of
then we add [somewhere] term? a
then we add [somewhere] of not exist but to God,
then we add [somewhere] exist but to
then we add [somewhere] and understanding
then we add [somewhere] or innovative poet, for
then we add [somewhere] a venue for
then we add [somewhere] there are reality

then we add [somewhere] loves then, and
then we add [somewhere] then, is the poet
then we add [somewhere] itself. as a means
then we add [somewhere] language
then we add [somewhere] ends in reality, are
then we add [somewhere] idealist
then we add [somewhere] the gods, the oracles?
then we add [somewhere] a poet who
then we add [somewhere] are there not;
then we add [somewhere] gods, he
then we add [somewhere] brand
then we add [somewhere] unclear ends in
then we add [somewhere] as an
then we add [somewhere] , lack of a poet

VII.

love ends at/
toward an
unclear end. why,

then must the poem
be a false awareness

an understanding
that does not exist

but to God, oracles

then is the poet, or
innovative poet,
for lack of a better
poet, languaging
an end in itself

[a means toward an
unclear end

a venue for/
of the false].

VIII.

dogs are in the mirror

no an unconventional mirror

does not mean I AM A DOG or I SEE MYSELF
REFLECTED
         AS ONE

rather, the *Atlas of the Human Body*
lay unflipped
on a temporary table
otherwise known as my ironing board

carpal tunnel, carpal tunnel

Ethan Paquin is an aggregate
of sinew and worn things
that wrinkle easily

Lax Lax

i.	ii.	iii.
no	what	so
bet	do	a
ter	st	story
place	you	of
to	attempt	dis
start	to	sip
than	teach	ation
the	me?	, dis
mini	Robt	appear
mal	Lax,	ance
ism	how	begin
mal	can	neth
a	the	here,
prop	hermit	for
ism	teach	Lax
dr	anyway	doth
glock	—hobb	sym
enspie	led	bol
l's	by	ise
style	his	my
mean	hid	gam
der	ing	bit
ing	ren	—o
sun	der	how
in	ed	the
ton	an	thin
ing	un	neth
pebbles	reli	row
—	able	of
dribb	nar	word
ling	rat	be

caries
of
the
stag
nant
pond,
pretty,
black
as
some
gone
shoal

or
by
his
reluc
tant
narra
tiv
ity
and
nar
ra
tion

the
viol
ent
est
type.
see
the
blank
ness?
i'm
in
it

Guidance

i'm in it

— <a> wrote:
>
> E,
>
> Why do you like that painting—
> it is only a colour field?

>

> A
>
>
>—— Original Message——
> From: "<Ethan Paquin>"
> To: "<a>"
> Sent: Saturday, November.
> Subject: Re: professor/lax
>
>
> > a,
> >
> > the oil is in relief, like lax. let me explain—my
> > professor friend teaches English and is a painter
> > in his spare time, so I think his literary influences
> > really shine through in his visual work. the way
> > the oil paint is beaded across the canvas is like he
> > read dr. glockenspiel and said 'I want to imitate
> > the monosyllabic via paint.' there you go... —
> > suffice to say if you place a paint decoder against
> > one of his pieces, you will hear an eerie banging
> > of coffins—'in here! in here!'
> >

> > to yr wellness,
　　> >
　　> > e
　　> >
　　> >— <a> wrote:
　　> > >
> > > Ethan,
　　> > >
　　> > > I need somewhere to begin

What is Language? [I]

i.	ii.	iii.
What	She	I
is	Because	ear
language?	she	-marked
I	loves	his
want	me	"Page
to	Becomes	62"
craft	my	or
This	word.	is
as	My.	it
simply	Mine.	the
as	Love.	publisher's
possible.	Lover.	"Page
But	She	62"
simple	is	?
is	my	At
not	little	any
possible	day	rate
because	book	I
I	full	had
don't	of	been
know	my	filled
where	scribblings.	Had
I	And	been
am.	it	consumed
Having	is	Had
read	all	been
his	becoming	in
books	so	And
I	clear	now
am	—moon	am
the	by	of

[18]

noun
of
another,
his
one
grand
text.

lamp-light,
ficus
in
morn-light
—no-one
owns
herself.

and
by
that
thing
called
"Page
62."

What is Language? [II]

i.	ii.	iii.
Listen:	I	Listen:
Need	do	
to	not	
believe	borrow	
you'll	Lax	
come	I	
and	am	
find	Lax	
me.	I	
Here,	am	
where	no	
I	Ethan	
am.	that	
Wherever	is	
I	for	
am.	sure.	
I've	Ethan	
been	would	
to	never	
some	have	
odd	written	
places.[1]	like	
Are	this	Are
you	Ethan	you
listening	may	listening
to	never	to
"me"	have	"me"
or	written	or
to	at	to
"Lax"?	all.	"Lax"?

[1] Lax, from *Psalm*, pp. 6 (UK: Stride, 1991)

[20]

Wherefore Breeze?

i.	*ii.*	*iii.*
To	To	The
breake	a	muchly
(witness:	vessel	white
how	clean	between
the	(take	words
book	*i.* :	Between
be	with	columns
placed	no	Between
down	book	stanzae
and	I	Bloweth
I	had	here
sat	only	This
more	the	winding
up	day	Leaf
whence	which	Much
the	is	like
breezes	to	a
began,	say	garden
for	only	:
it	green	Something
was	maybe	with
was	blue	which
so	/gray,	To
calming	mireless	birth

Simplicity

i.	ii.	iii.	iv.
Do	Do	Why	Why
you	I	do	write
love	happyn	I	like
me?	you?	read?	this?
Why	If	Why	What
do	I	do	are
I	do,	I	the
ask?	why?	write?	answers?
Can	Why	What	Are
I	do	am	the
trust	you	I	answers
it?	answer?	after?	mine?
Can	Can	Why	What
I	you	write	is
love	read	about	mine,
you?	eyes?	love?	afterall?

"Simplicity" through the Logotex

　　　　　[It] happyn[s]　　　　　I　　like
me[.]　　　　　　　　　[* * *]　　[Me?] [Y]ou?　　　　　　[R]ead?
[T]his?　[A]fter [ ]
[/] all[,] [it's]

[w]hy　　[i]f [you like me, you like my library.]　　　　[* * *]　　Why
do　　　[you] [d]o [that,] [/]
[think about me as *sui generis*?] [* * *]
　　　　　　　　　　　　　　　　　　[Yes, I]　[d]o [like me,]
　　　　[w]hy[?]　　　　　　　　　　　What [do]
you　　　　　　[c]are [what I]　　　　　　write?
I　　　　　　　　　　　　do[ ] [know]　　　　　　　　　I
　　　　[am to me]　　　　　the
[greatest question] ask[ed.]　　　　　　　　　Wh[at]　　　about
　　　　[me is]　　　　　mine,
you?　　　　　　　　　　　　　　　　　[My] eyes?
　　　　[Your] love?　　　　　　　　　　　　[His] answers? [*
　　　* *]
I　　　　　　　　　　　　　do　　　　　　　write [−]
　　　　　　[w]hy[,]　　　　　　　　[w]hat[?]
Are ["]I["] [and] ["]love["] [motivatours, and if so,]

　　　　why?　　　　　　　　　　　[I]
[c]an　　　do[ubt]　　　answers[;]　　[I] am　　　the
[author]　　　　[thank] you[for clarifying−I am the *reader*.]
　　　　[Get]
it?　　　　　　　　　　[Got] answer[s]?
[Chapter] after?　　[* * *]　　[M]ine
　　　　　　　　　　[words, not to]　　trust[, e'er.]
Can[not, absolutely]　　　Can[not trust them.]
Why[, you ask]　　　　　　　I　　do [not exist.]
What I ["am," is]
["]I["][,] [an aggregate.]　　　　[Y]ou [see,]　　　　　　[the]
writ[ten]　　　　　　　　[ha]s [thiev'ed me]　　[* * *]
["me"] [you] love　　　　　　　　[to] read

Missive

> > > arc of a chapter/arc of a life?
> > >
> >
> >
> > We artists—all borrowers, none of us "us" so none of us
> > special?
> >
> > Is that what you mean?
> > We shd all give up—
> >
> > <i>Blunt'd arcs, and abounding</i> - Anon.
> >
> >
> >
> >
> >
> >

More of the Monologue

Scathalogue

Dire, the minimalism of a tornado watch map
which is the most confident of paintings, yes.

All the dots where potential tornadoes may turn up—
I have seen those fields last year, never saw their tinge

of tractor, only the blought of air ready to go east
and bring some loose sands and grasses with it.

When walking by these fields I try to see them
yellowed, like adulterated photos. The greens

more brilliantly washing into the redder sky,
browner edges of clouds that want little to do

with time—to be as careless as a damn cloud,
yep, my first and best thought here on the bluff

and once on a Caribbean cliff, in Maine once
in a tidal basin near The Nonantum, up high

atop a peak known since the 1890s as Owl's Head—
always the clouds most interesting, always needing

them to be perfecter, wanting them different ways,
fascinated by their names, the Latinate, their dying

over Newfoundland but never Florida, place worthy
not of my dreams or attentions or fancies. Clouds,

most confident of installation pieces, yes. The world
a gallery, really, and all I can find the time to do:

waste time with words, ignored little bastards, think
of the wasted efforts, all those basement storage books

gone, hidden, gone efforts, think *don't authors know,*
clouds and maps confront us daily, succinctly.

Towers of Buffalo

Today I return to writing because I saw high spires and smoke-
stacks, and they were the kind that made my mouth water for
being important—so stark and blasted, dropped terra cotta
on some onyxified craterscape, everyone holding hands
in little circles and approaching carefully, awfully big and bold-
fucking God out of the sky. Those towers near Johnson Park,
the ovular neighborhood near the party district overlooking grass
and courtyards and which is filled with mansards and hipped
rooves . . . and Delaware Avenue, *its* various towers. So the act of
seeing towers has led me to my chair and my pen, tricked me in-
to thinking there is anything more—those structures are what's
impressive. How can any writing man touch what it is about him
that makes him a man, when it's all there, coursing through that
stonemasonry—dead stuff to the naked eye of the American Dolt,
but the gaping mouthwatering challenging welcoming woman to
the artist.

Yes, I am an Artist

these were the famous words of someone I know whose name I
forgot because he made nothing

these were the famous words of someone I know whose name I
forgot because he made nothing

made nothing know
whose name I forgot because he made nothing
I because he made nothing   someone I   because he
know these
were the   I know whose name I forgot because
he made nothing
these were the famous words of someone forgot   whose
name
these were the famous words of someone I know because I forgot
famous words of I
these were the famous words of someone

Adolph Gottlieb to the Little Animals

brother mine the crab, *Untitled* 1973

brother mine the sand, *Echo* 1972

brother mine the thistle, *Brink* 1959

brother mine the blood, *Crimson Ground* 1972

brother mine the borealis, *Blue Night* 1970

brother mine the sand dollar and the ray

the eel and the mantis

the bat and the rathawk

and the rat

      ~

(further up) the bat

                        the rathawk
                        the rat

(further in) the mantis

                (further out) the sand dollar

                    (further down) the ray
                    (further down) the eel

Brother

brother mine the crab,

brother mine the sand,

brother mine the thistle,

brother mine the blood,

brother mine the borealis,

brother mine the sand dollar and the ray

    the eel and the mantis

the bat and the rathawk

and the rat

    ~

(further up) the bat

                              the rathawk
                              the rat

(further in) the mantis

                  (further out) the sand dollar

                        (further down) the ray
                        (further down) the eel

Tigers

The paint stethoscope revealed:

      the tiger. Here!   He was placed by a benign hand in
gentle ochres,

is restored in the museum that's identical to other museums

by a man who: drank coffee for lunch and: wants tapas with
Johanna after work;

Johanna's face reminds him how perfect the painting was, once,
drying on an easel,

    how perfect things are really clotheslines with day-one-clean
shirts,

and you see where this metaphor is going, especially if the
metascene occurreth:

in a Great Lakes city, where mum is the malevolent wind, thunder,

mum like all great enemies biding time in all the hidden pores.

Why Do I Wait for the Thunder Nightly

At the end of a twelve-foot-wide hallway
there is one of my windows.

And at the end of that one of dozens
of windows, a deveined pocket of dark.

Within, the shakening shudder of elm,
only I don't see it this way or at all:

there are highlight lines the moving leaf
of midnight. Makes. The leaves make

me want the thunder, which has held off
as a tanker ship abandoned in shallows

at some washed, eighty-foot-high dry dock
where everyone stays away from sadness

has handed itself its death settle — can you
imagine the loss of floating on the sea?

Whether the tanker ship does, or thunder
imagines loss . . . of itself, perhaps, for

after all, it is the fadingest of all murders,
murder of ion and calm, of brown sky,

there are crumpled circles, cats-eyes, almost,
rolled to the end of that hallway, bunched

in the left corner. I want to reach out,
to palm the marbles near a sullen rain.

I Found the Reason for the Tree

When all had failed and left with night

when perch an utmost blueness sought

when blue the cryolesce besot

I'd satten there and thence before,

yet never this inspi'red as.

I found the reason for the tree;

I found the reason for the tree.

Blue Composition Bombing

The nightmare of weight the nightmare of balance nearnt,
but I wouldn't stop it from coming
                                        [I looked down on me in my sleep
, ready to absorb it] because a painting was no dearth ratio

of sea to cloud absorb'ed but how

for a vulgarity

in poetry

to blast itself upon me and you?   When?

                    Did you happen to see the new sign I spit upon?

I am now wanting the page to be wider than eighty-three absolutely putrid
        gourmands,

so I may place the words anywhere.

This is why poetry is lacking, is confinement, is why it's no longer.

On the distant lake shore, she waits. [She longs.]

On the distant lake shore, the woman I loved waits. [I loved, she longs, she
        "nears."]

On the distant lake shore, the woman I loved waits for the novel ending.
[I loved, she longs, she's "nearer"
            yet also as you see my words creating the panscape,
    over the unknown and unnamed lake [[context clue: elsewhere in the chapter:
        'Great Lakes']] and swooping down to her sadly face,
            she becomes less knowable—a cipherature for the mitigance—
we know our hum for it's on our lips but that it is something dead
    is what not
            escapes us, just as now you realize: "the woman"'s a ballast
                for the camera known as the poem]

On the distance to the lake the promise of shore, the pout of dead bird,
the lap of sickly language of a polluted wave tabulature.

Any attempt at a novel ending with lovely cacciatore is pure sermon,

that thing only levied at us but hardly the wine we'd want chilled
on our behalves.   So pointless.   Go toward a forty-five degree grain elevator.

This is why it's read no longer:

my thoughts make less sense than yours.

The flower looks prettier than the hovering circles, yes?

Ekphratica

Considerations of things physical and human,
that consideration of minimalism and balance,

Friday morning with art in mind. Battened by
burdensome and clunky syllably and syntac-

tical gestures, a washed-with-the-daylights poet
returned from a visit to a gallery of sculpture,

having walked there with his son in a rain made
half-palatable by easy cadence, and morning's Friday,

and those considerations all. All wrapt up in premises
. . . the stillness within the menace of one's pictographs,

the wisdom within another's columnar, monosyllabic
meander—like a grade-school poem-corpse rendered

on some academy frontlawn: combining simple words,
the children end with a creation, a thing chromey

or cloudy . . . as when one mistakes into a village garden,
and is stunned by bulbs from nowhere else, and there-

in, some way of light is discovered. Paint-stick scribble,
dappled childsong (dappled with air, spaces. The child

peering the corner at a cat, discovered.), new ways of light
and gravity. Words hanging in heavy spaces of blank,

one stroke lost among stroke among all other strokes—
no matter the much-different method, there's a flower

to the left of the son who walks in cadence with his father,
and it doesn't sound like a poem or look like a painting.

Continae

I have become that old man we
all know from elsewhere: the
peek out the front door, count
antpairs til the next breeze. My
canvas waits in the attic, hung
for eight days with a gesso not
yet readied, the ideas elsewhere.
Every leaf so bright, but there's
nothing to paint and no senti-
ment but the want of a giant
gust to make all the much-
needed changes.

The wait for my wife, like eras-
ing words backwards — novella
gotten down to its first thou-
sand words. I am nothing but a
series of long processes — night
time, hating words, alone in
bed, the boating trip taken once
in some other state in which we
would not be apart.

We know we love each other for
we wish we loved each other
more. If we were not in love we
would wish for things as easy as
tin, bark, spokes. Simplesse. I
know I love her for I wish I loved
her more.

My neighbour is an old man
with no hat, no smock, no large
equations on his mind. I can
only assume the latter. In and by
assuming, I know I have lost
some of the lonelitinge. In and
by looking at my old neighbour,
I know he is at least slightly
aware of my presence, there on
my porch, peering over at him.
It may make him angry, it may
not.

She has not written in a week,
so I must have made her angry.
It is a strange, cobbled district:
to be on your own mind, but not
on her mind. I hope for light-
ning—it always comes at five.

What will her face do when she
arrives back, what will my first
stroke resemble. Only now are
these things bigger than every-
thing. Only on a day adress with
before-thunder, wind's promise
for something, do the small
things stand out—contrasts,
nothing more than those, e.g. as
Rothko has made us notice.

Era of too-tired-for-punctuation.
I want to hate the machines
spilling everything, making this
daylight so goddamned . . . dire.
Wheels, sockets, mortar drills, a
dangling lightsline. But the new
sunroom has been inhabited for
the month. Daily a new spider
web, daily the spider's chance to
walk on an air she hasn't before
touched.

Stills

Tried with a wind to aid but no paint would apply   none
    how is a cloud gotten?   how does the painter become large
like the stellar things.

     ~

Does he posit a subtext near the face of his wife   by
    a green hemiwindow?   a curtain swayeth becomes bold
and her hair stands out as a still swing.

     ~

Beauty is perhaps a word we like   choice
    lodges in cold attics?   slip on socks to up there trudge,
retreive the little iron box.

Nothing But Setting Out

Rothko has made us notice daily
the spider's chance —

hating words,
she has not written in a week.

Old man with no hat, no smock,
eight days with a gesso not yet readied,

in some other state is
every leaf so bright. Is sunrooms, tin.

Large equations: the peek out the front door,
each boating trip a series of long processes.

Beautiful Nighttime Churches

Made whiter by spotlight, like a canoe dotting the transcript that's a
      muddy, winding river—
like one outside a town called Canajoharie, New York, by which
      alongside a bridle path:
a strange one-storeyed gate house of sorts, with two-storey-tall windows,
      the whole thing
whitewashed, a gate beyond, and then, the dotted and muddied and
      windening river—
if the canoe be seen by moonlight. There may be islands in that river,
      trees bowing over
into shallows to catch a better view of a sort of sentinel white—
      birchy canoe, no one in it
or near it. No one near the gate house, no one touched by October by
      its gate. And by that
one means, this is the point where a year turns on its

      he was killing bugs outside
and now he's writing their body parts down. What comes after r?
      Arrows pointing I made
arrows pointing to everything. What else can we find to make a label
      for? They probably
they probably ate the worm over midnight   *Right?*
                  and by that one means, this is the point where a
child turns on its parent   crude forerunner to husband or wife
and by that one left cut down, the bowing grandparent
means, this is the point where a conversation turns
on its
where a scene turns on its
where a thing like a star turns on its
where a beautiful nighttime church burns on its foundation   And one
realises: the two-storey gate house will be a postscript   will be a
      painting one

day: at dusk, the two-storey gate house is not as white as the
       church's facade:
green town common, strobe of white making a church facade
       gleam:
the canoe just may be whiter than the church

Modillion Modillion Modillion

White is a long process, I think. She is scraping mortar from a tile
floor next door.
Porcelain octagon   Porcelain octagon   Porcelain octagon

I hear in the spaces an arduous effort of chipping then sweeping
as I write / the page is white but becoming less so.

I walk side streets and the day is not foliage or gray or curb but dentil
modillion bay and turret. God, the canvases are so damned full,
the spaces are filled up and it makes
one stop and take pause of what he is about to write—will it
suffice, does it add to the world, or just
clutter things up beyond repair.

                    and maybe the troublesome thing is the "beyond
                    repair"—
                    i believe i learned paint could be scraped away,
                    words erased homes burned
                    if that were meted.

                    still the damages abound
                    (threat of damages abound)

stilly a slow cloud a slow cloud presently vapourises Buffalo Harbour

Axis of Minimal

I wanted to see in glass stones.
A stranger, riding into the woods.
View of branches.
No far off bay.
A horse.
How strangers tuck a hand more gently than most people do, and
where they tuck their hand is clear
inside in their pocket.
How strangers tuck a hand more gently than most people do, and
where they tuck their hand is clear
inside in their pocket.
How on a bay lined with the detritus of branches thrown across the
stones we have the essence of a
nomad.
How on a bay lined with the detritus of branches thrown across the
stones we have the essence of a
nomad.
How a far off bay's wintered by woods and glass. Glassed in by
woods.
Horses feel about with weary hooves.
They see the branches and the bay.

Hampton

Come see what I'm doing: writing this
beach, staring its lines. I can hold a banana
to the shoreline and, with one eye squinted
shut, match the curves of the fruit and coast.
The waves, then, lap against the peel. Rocks,
then, bolster the peel—they look like gathered
friends. Else they assault the peel—they swarm
about. But, truly, all is harmless right now—tide,
even. It is nearly newspaper time. It is nearly clip
of boulder. Peripherally, a sand and another sand.
Peripherally, once, the kite. Orange. Far above
Boar's Head, a jetty whereon the wealthy perch
for coffees and viewpoints jockeyed. Build higher,
convert—a motel to a condo, a home to a home
of some larger species, braideled with vinyl else
other very white contraptions. Where the organic?
Buoys, still enmeshed by thousands of feet of rope,
seablast walls of weathered concrete. This is called:
point of death, that is called: point of lifeline.
Hovering, wind's east tidal—makes it all natural,
kills foam of buoy mesh of thick poly lobster-trap-
cord smalls smell of coconut jelly applique applied
and bolstered by this flight of gray I walk, nearing.
The clump of rock, patch thirty yards out, The Island.
I have a figure who walks out to it with a plastic bag,
stoops there while, for instance, a solitary dog chases
a ball—a man tosses a ball. Stoops there, slightly moving—
the distant view of a woman in baggy brown, hair and cloth
blought, slightly adjusting one wrist—wee pulnar twitches,
carpal twinges, whatever those muscles are, by this figure
brown and far-off. For instance, I watch her from the seawall—
graffitoed by wintercrack and moss cluster, patched in spots
by diligent state workers, now likely huddled at home—after
all, it is November. After all, it is New Hampshire. After all

the rain this season, it may be uncharacteristically warm, yet one
worker said to his colleague, his friend-of-34 years, perhaps, who'd
walked with him along many many miles of beaches poking trash
and discarding it in many many battered green Park System barrels,
I don't trust God so I don't trust anything, not even the skies, those
damn things'll open when they please. The friend-of-34-years may say,
may have to pull out his toothpick to do so, *Sure, like on Mount Clay*
that one day—remember, after the wedding rehearsal? Drive home,
slap those boots on, drive to Vermont, cheap hotel, cross Connecticut
again to Twin Mountain and beyond, skies—man, Goddamned blue,
colder than that, even. I remember—do you? It was warm, is the short
of it. I recall the range looming over the dashboard. Felt out of place,
wished the highway was gone. Removed. Then I could tell—the rain
was raining in Vermont, over its large little lake, which appears on maps
as a body of considerable size yet is crossed by boat in several minutes
—in certain spots, I mean—in other spots deep and full of dead deer
—and that rain would make it here. For the wedding, too. So we made
time to the trailhead, sun was risen, and you shouted, Come see! And hell,
all the mud. But, remember we went up? Sun was risen but tenuous   sun was
nodding, sun was   Yep, keep coming . . .   we walked and the rain
and the rain   and the rain was. We couldn't make the summit. I tripped
on the way down, you couldn't catch me. Shit. Tripped for the first time
ever on a hike, ever. And you witnessed it. Remember, we laughed? We did,
at the wedding. The wedding was something. Toothpick again. *Whose, again?*
The friend-of-34-years says more than the other, but the other's eyes
fix nowhere else but on his colleague, who has convinced him and utterly:
We're staying in today. Weekend cards, smokes. Fireplace, wood in the cellar
in the corner. His eyes appreciate friend-of-34-yearses level of detail (less than
this poet uses to relate the conversation, decidedly more than the stereo-
typed grumblings of middle-class, well-past-middle-age state Park System
workers). Let's bring up some wood. And it keeps rushing back—the trail's
roots, smell of height, the only-one-place-ever feel of skylight streaming aface
from betwixt the conflated branches of krummholz and beaten summit
spruce. Yes, they are close friends, and good workers. Articulate men, one

reads Keats and the other, something by Elias. The friend-of-34-years has a way of finding—always with a toothpick amouth, always with the other by his side and whistling, inths of wrapper litter flitting along the sand, half-buried bottles. He looks for and through the bottles—green or brown ways of seeing the Isles of Shoals, written about so much, studied by scientists, but to no one else the place of birds that heralded the washed-up corpse of his eight-year-old neighbour boy. The child was a bad one, indeed, breaking windows with baseballs and feeling no remorse, running through flower gardens on Emerald Lane in Hampton, small side street of the out-there world in which New York City is some be-all and end-all, but to those with true senses of smell and an inner life, no good place to be, frankly—the child, yes —his name was not Frankie, his birthplace not New York, but here— village center called Harvey, a red place in spring. That's all one need know about the child's birth: his mother, prettied with black hair, picked various roses in her neighbourhood side streets and became enamoured of another neighbour, and then a bouquet of roses on a mahogany table; an oil-heat bill each month; a raked yard. A child—playing on Emerald Avenue, some years removed from various roses and then, it was quickly over: he was plucked by a rapist, heaved in a trunk full of must and locked therein and   with the rapist helped by rapist accomplices tossed over a one-car bridge   into a dwindling mud tide   and the hours did pass   and passed and the child was forgotten, really— crushed daisies   window shards, tenuous ready to drop from sills   clouds and hues of gray passed   but he was long dead, really. No drama in cloudpass or fractured images of things holding on, Hope seated at the dinner table, child barging in and the "Where were you, son?"—really, it was too late for that scene to ever play out. And the rapist and his friends, maybe two of them, are off somewhere unknown—like Chile, but in Maine. Like China, but in Presque Isle, drinking quarter brews in a border bar and set in purpose, set to hike into Quebec to a cabin, beneath which are various bones: come see, come see. The friend-of-34-years leans back in a chair in front of a fire, that's all. Follow its smoke . . . over the low hills. Nowhere near the seawall, nowhere near now, which I am nearing. My figure and far off, watched for days in a row. So, the dog runs about her, maybe wearing a handkerchief; the ball scoots away from the dog; the ball was thrown by one man. The waves are coming and now faster. The banana I've half-eaten. The clouds still generate. The gulls, of course. The grays, of course. The flapping of flags and lawns, the high homes of Boar's Head, of course. The rotting boy and the rotting islands, the aging workers and the litter, all the litter flying. But here I am, studying the wrist of the figure, my one and favourite human —in brown, she stands out, although The Island is brown and the mood is slightly as dun as brown. The banana is browning. Bones are browning. The day, too, shuttles onward toward a future known as overripe, which will birth a new day which will be yet another day in which an eight-year-old boy's bones rot in a sink-hole, an eight-year-old boy's parents shift table runners and vases to forget about loss, an eight-year-old-boy's neighbour enjoys scraping toothpick from between his teeth, an eight-year-old boy's plundered garden plants re-grow at the fissures and fractures, an eight-year-old boy's rapist hides in a forest cabin dreaming of raping eight-year-old boys. In this breeze, in this November, it may be a balmy day, but this banana is browning, the shoreline is no longer the same shape as minutes pass by, I am no nearer The Island or the figure for the former recedes into higher tide and the latter just keeps wandering. She has a plastic bag and there is a reason: she collects shells. No type of shell in part- icular, but the more intact, the better. She uses them for her garden— crunches them and makes walkways through her herbs. One can list varieties of herbs—fennel, borage, chervil— and one can list varieties of Atlantic shells—scallop, mussel, quahog—but whether one can list every moment that ever led to this figure, this woman, wanting to become someone who collected shells with which to dust her garden pathway, one can't be sure. Whether one can connect her dollhouse to her rabbit coop to kickball to sweet sixteen to american pie to beer blast to beloved husband til death do her   part of a lifetime contract to give up dreams of interior design and poetry writing   to child one unwanted error but loved anyway to child two to home one and two and three to this shore eventually, after no major deaths in the family and yards of antique and ribbon and hemlock brush behind home three, a nineteenth century farmhouse near this shore   upon which she decided, *I need to keep returning here* and maybe *I need to be good* too and, perhaps, *Come see, dear, come see this shell   oh, what striping I love it I love you I love the view the Isles of Shoals*, one can't be comfortable with that outlook. And there she goes, slowly, brown and blowing in this breeze, to the left: the north: a tidal pool: just like her: small element of the vaster landscape, micron, "the mote." Here is her leaning, her stooping; the flags blast behind me: west: never stopping, the tide keeps rising, the day keeps darkening, speed of the dog and the ball, speed of the thoughts of the man who owns the dog: *I want to hold my wife right now. I want to buy cheese and eat slowly with her. Whether listing every cheese I know—washed rind, cooked—will help me decide what to do with the rest of this weekend, I know not. Whether that woman over there is going to go home, because it's cooling down and because the sun is receding into less-than.* Here is the dog. *Here is my dog. He goes. Always a 'going' in the bones of the dog.* Here is my figure, line of the arch of her back in concert with the rock of the outline of Boar's Head. Blowing of her hair in concert with the way that wave gathers and melts, the way that one. Not that. Whip of her hair, its curly manner of blowing—in toward her forehead, then out toward the boats   whip of the flags to the west. Sine. The dog, his red scarf. His belief system, his instinct,

the propellor of mud down a ravine in autumn. Red scarf to the
north, red scarf to the south, red scarf intersect the belly of my
figure, red scarf obscure The Island, red scarf back again and back
to its intersection—favourite act of the gods of aesthetics. "Here is
a scene, here now is its unsettling. Here is an object, here is its
shuttling and how you must understand: nothing is ever as you
want it. The scarf will move for it is attached to the nape of a
dog. The dog, you know it will move. And by its moving the
scene is altered: now, understand. Create, or go home, get off this
seawall, don't lean on it and keep staring at the woman, shells,
shells in her pouch." I understand the intersection, men; after
all, I began this creation. Ahem, I began this creation with the act
of lining up one object with another object: interplay, at least, if
not intersection. The interplay of a banana's curve and a shore-
line's—nothing radical at all. Elementary, even. Squint and see
things anew. Remember that murder scene? It really happened.
Intersection: of beach and correlating notions of: American
leisure and frivolity and vanity, banality of American painting
and photography wherein the island on the beach horizon is
framed dead-center and the birds above upper-right-hand-corner:
with: On That Island, A Child Was Tortured. I understand, men.
Red scarf of the dog, inertial beast! Red scarf of the man of
cheese, the man of beaten wife, who is likely in the tub right now
feeling her thigh—wiping him off her. Intersection of (a) that
man and (b) that that man is HERE and (c) that he could be some-
where else, he's got a wedding band on, but he's here, and with a
look: *My dog. He goes. I want to go—but can't, just yet. Maybe her
boyfriend will be there . . . . . . I recall the way her hand totally and
mechanically contracted upon the blast of a wave sloshing her bare ankle
—the crush and cringe, flesh versus muscle and the "Oh!" with smile in
the littoral zone.* : and (d) this is a beach. Come see. My figure has
this one tic: and I'm thinking of this only because she isn't doing
it, but likely will momentarily: she will, after crouching into the

direction of the tidal pool at hand, hand gone in and hand come out with shell, hold the shell aloft like it was a coin . . . with thumb and fore- thought, and one finger, pinch the shell, squinting at it; *is it cracked?, is it more perfect than Asia?.* . . . draw it nearer her face, still squinting at the catch. . . . carefully, then, open her plastic bag, which is by one handle drooping from her right forearm, same arm as the hand that inspects, with her left hand; take the shell in her left hand, wedding band glinting but only as much as a shard of mug on a sidewalk for she has been married long; and head into the bag, hand gone in hand come out with no shell. . . . place the shell pile of shell pile of shells. Placed the shell. Now will she do this one thing that, frankly, moves me to a kind of point of hilarity. Not that what she does is funny, or what she looks like is funny . . . but that a person is, and is these movements, and is at the same time such a large no. I know her not; I don't really ever see her eyes. I can't say how often she comes here. Or how often, less often she will want to as dogs go by. I like this: she unbends her knees and decrouches and always with her left hand after shell-poaching boofs the sand and sea from her sweater. Grab the sweater with thumb and finger, pull outward pull outward pull outward. As if a man trying violently to pry a nail from driftwood—nail somewhat insecure in its hole, wood somewhat spongy, but no give either way. I think it's apparent she hates sand on her sweater; is it an important sweater, an un- important sand, etc. Intersection of observation and assumption. Red scarf, red gift . . . ? Yellow labrador dog, because a black labrador wasn't available at the kennel . . . ? Hampton, intersection of Route 1 and one of the "letter streets"—Avenue A and on and on, the seablast wall and the figure, the impending next day and the banana eaten. Lines. Linesphere. Shapes and things less made, like mentionings and rumblings—mud sloughing off a tidal ditch one mile away, parka ruffling gainst the body of a walker, bottle settling in the trash can near the pizza crust. Gull skeleton, inorganic buoy foam, cigarette filters. Nighttime encroaching, but I haven't been here for more than a few sentences — very long ones. These hours . . . the man has gone, with his dog. My figure walked north and away and into tomorrow's shell hunt, if she comes, and maybe I won't come to see it. Her tic did not come. Maybe the seawall will not stand but I am sure it will; a safe very safe assumption. It is cracked, but minorly and patched with less-than-superior skill (mortar is chafing away; someone has shoved a straw in one of the cracks) but, one day will die and the next will come and we learn from stasis: the beach is there, more or less, the water is there, the gray may not be there at four but will at some other hour and the wall is there, keeping people on the boardwalk from being harmed by waves, and the wall will be there. It is like a felled log on Mount Clay: *how long has it been here?* It is keeping people looking and leaning out. Come see, come see.

Peripherally: Boar's Head. Walk there — it's nothing like the palatial gardens of the big ski resort in Vermont, like the gleaming rubber mountaintop of Hiram Dump. What it offers is a reprieve from: sand: wind: run-down cottages of the letter streets. Walk there: you'll see. I before E, except after C the lawns get more manicured and the people, more tolerable in their choice of candidates and shutter colours. Come see: if I align the banana's curve with the shoreline, the tip of the banana — where it was once attached to the tree — points east, directly away from this area of cottages. The end-end of the banana too goes out to sea, on a line never to return/ to connect with shrimpers. The lines of a banana at night are difficult, in ways . . . yellow is always yellow, whether or not there's a street lamp beaming down, and it nearly glows. Back- ground, gone into black. So one can stand there, banana to face with squinted eye trying to see how the universe is oriented and things connected, looking foolish. Night time, black Hampton, rush of ocean beyond the sea wall, having stood there for hours just looking out, yellow fruit yellow form hovering in the black. Nameless black; faceless figure. Faceless bones, out there and buried somewhere. Faceless killers, faceless kites faceless wives   *Dear, you out of the bath yet?*   *The dog got into some kelp or some shit Honey when will the flowers grow back that kid trampled them Hey I will put this knife up there if I want to No I need shells the old ones with which I paved the path are too gritty too small I will go to The Island tomorrow and gather some more Come see how this woman places herself on the landscape, places shells in a cheap plastic bag Fetch! Fetch!   No don't get into the You're gonna fall if you climb on that jetty, get down here Rub this on my back Grab that bottle Yeah that one Goddamned kids didn't anyone ever teach them to not litter Remember how the sky remember how the sun Remember how we drove in the rain and nearly didn't make it Remember gods of aesthetics I am only a novice. I never said this was a masterful poem Yes I made fun of the painters and photo artists who crop shots perfectly, you gotta admit it's pretty banal stuff And what if I told you, the figure was my mother?* And what if I told you I live nowhere near nearing this scene, hundreds of miles off where ocean is an idea like a banana tree — who the hell has ever seen a banana tree, certainly no one I know. They can't even afford to pay the rent, they have no chance of going to the Dominican. They dream of Chile and see some air in their heads and when we dream we all have the air in our heads seemingly tinted . . . and when we make mention of all the various roses, we flex awareness of there's more than one ocean We nod to our friends and how they uncork wine bottles using unconventional methods We feel warmth for never having been kidnapped and pillaged with fireplace machines like pokers and stokers   We feel like we can go over to wherever we want and stare out, trying to sense the blue between a middling white and gray. Come see — and what if I couched this all by saying, the wake was held for that figure some twenty-seven years from now, and the only people who showed up were herb garden enthusiasts

Would the seawall take on some sadliness, or, yes, The Island become a sort of without flag pole? Twenty-seven years from now, an herb grower in green (a frock) and one in pink (a gown) will throw hibiscus on the figure's coffin   or could will throw hibiscus on the figure's coffin In green the sentiment, maybe she didn't like to be that way In pink I knew her mother, suffered so In all in all A chorale, o the ocean is vocal o the fields of flowers is all In all in all nowhere, the Park System friends; the snap't rose; the box- stuffed bruise known as the murder. The men who hiked together died years hence, the dog chasing a ball with his gaudy scarf made friends with a cat who once killed sixteen chipmunks in his career as cat and they snuggled incessantly. The wife took baths forever. Her husband found a mint on her pillow and he was the one who left it there. She did not take it. So yes he continued walking the beach at Hampton, alone. His next dog was a lap dog and boring. In all in all the seawall stood, would not give. Over the aeons known as birthdays, successive watchers came. One had a name whose name started with an S.

Towrd a Shoreline

(to be moaned)

come-a walk along the stones

       come-a clear the doe from the highway,
her teeth as small as childrens' chariots

come-a spend your life among the pilings

       come-a far above our little city, come up,
your fear as dulled as garnets

come-a mine this midnight's loudness

       come-a hollow out this pumpkin,
make eyes from mama's amulets

the doe, her eyes as dull as amulets . . .

midnight's little city . . .

The Exhibit

Carrying a citron purse, a woman walks into landscape
in Maine. Walks toward a museum, toward the exhibit
therein. Looks intent on discovering things not even
the painters of the great works to be seen in the show
could see. One knows she is intent for she has no hitch,
no pause for the blue jay over the campus belfry—belfry
to the east, atop some hall, belfry to the west, benefactor
and benefactress having paid for the rights for their names
to grace the thing, but as if any student of paleontology cares
who they were or that they are philanthropists and Nouveau
architecture buffs. The campus is, like others, a thud or sponge
at lunch time—deadened heap-ness, heaviness of quiet, heft
of everyone left, everyone not on a quad or near a belfried building
or sitting, smoking and lunching, on the brick walls or boulders
found in quartered garden spaces, the kinds lovers enter at eve
in order to kiss awhile, the kinds in which someone who loves
gum chews gum. The campus is awash in this type of slateity
but for the woman, whose bag is nothing less than a berry
if the campus be a hill—a broad, slowly-sloping-upward hill
that's uncanny. The berry bobs . . . moves ever onward, and one
sees the contrast between underripe forest berry, inedible, and hill
and blocks out everything else: the orange blob of bag becomes
the white bed in the Williams poem. The whole universe, it
seems to be all bed—it's given the title role, so to speak, it's
given ultimatism, so we the readers end there, on that image
and it is a grave, if slight, thing . . . universe as patrician bed,
done up in Chinese linens with lemons on the sideboards. Ah,
Williams got it right . . . there's nothing but objects on this play-
ing field, everything is to everything else a checker or thin, wafer-
ish game piece. And, here: the move is being made. The woman
saunters, bag swiffing confidently, ignoring the birds and the boys.
If one will take the opportunity to pan, one'll see a tall array of glass
breaking in one-third a several-storey box of pillars, a library?, or

something reminiscent of thought and study: Classical shrine, manuscript museum like the new one on the northwest corner of a rust belt city that gets no visitors but one, like with the name Theodora, and she wears vintage sandals and a less-than-dazzling sweater. It is the museum's glass. The woman reaches into her purse to extract a program. Correct—it is here, this is the . . . is the building, I wonder if Mara was right, if this will be worth it. She has a solid friendship: Mara, twenty-near years, has seen it all, from the woman- at-hand's failure at her first university to her basement apartment flood, Miss, you got roots growin in the plummin to the laughter to the buckets, all night the buckets. Dump the water, no, there in the street drain. How many cigarette quits? boyfriend splits and fucks, pregnancies dreamed and averted and wilfully forgotten? Camping trips to the Allagash, six hours up north, or Fort Mountain, where caught cold in a flash flood was some university professor, dead as gone lightning, or the Camden Hills? Twelve years and eighty-two hours after the crash, all night and half-naked in their off-campus apartment and the woman-at-hand threw up her tongue and Mara stuffed it back in, hid the pills the residue from Robert, the jealous boyfriend who would slap her if he found what Mara found: an ugly stash of some kind of Oregonian heavy metal, prescriptions stolen from Robert's grandmother's home in rural Vermont. Do you canoe? Robert and the woman-at-hand did, and she was so good he pushed her out and she died for seventeen seconds. For twelve of those, he stared at birds—four birds at first, then seven birds—the next five, he shook his dead girlfriend, and she awoke. So it went with the night Mara poked her entire forearm past the woman-at-hand's clenching throat muscles and esophagus, into the guts of the thing known as overdosing depressive young woman, and made sure to break her friend's ribs on the way out to keep it from all happening again. The woman awoke, hacking white cheek flesh, teeth contorted like jetties into the bedroom night,

Robert all bloodied and Mara's arm coated in smear, twelve years and eighty-two hours before. Now, on Mara's expert advice, the woman readies to enter a gallery to view Maine landscapes. Mara could have come but she was tending her sick mother, who sculpted and was shot with looks of hatred by little quaint people because she was a 'woman artist' and because she sculpted her best friend nude. She enjoyed firming the breasts and smoothing the belly; the clay gleamed in the afternoon. Session finished, the mother would help dress the model, sliding on her gown, the still life on her mind—seams and shadows of the gown against a background of sea, fluttering window dressing. And now, her life stilled like a dead trout run in the upwoods of Maine, where three people live, where six bridges bridge nine-hundred rivulets, where weakened moose and hikers are thrashed by torrents, the mother is bedded and sweatered in heavy woolen hand-me-downs, Mara's hands caressing the wrinkled cheeks, Mara's mind wandering to her friend having her day to herself at the gallery. The mother's work could have ended up on display there, but probably not. How many artists don't make it—their discoveries too bland like November weeks or mid-summer weeds, so the critics and curators take a pass. With her next five steps, the woman passes a large elm that was restored by tiny men in gabardines. Three gutted the trunk of turkey tail and bolete, both of which ate away at the sturdy pith of the old pioneer, some two-hundred years at that spot and counting. Two wrapped the fungus in newspaper, tossed at separate intervals (one worked faster than the other) the packs in a wheelbarrow, and hauled it all to some back angle of the campus, used it for fill. The tree, grateful, or at least one could imagine it would be, as one could imagine a child would be thrilled if a wasp was removed from his ear lobe, shuddered into a new kind of lifetime: one much more lusty, for the thing blew with a wondrous hiss during each windstorm, threw up its guard during each rainstorm, exuded like hell each autumn: little men in gabardines erected a kind of salvation. By carrying out their duties, fulfilling their custodial requirements, keeping the campus savory, they were ordinaries but also ecocentrists. However, the woman scantly notices the large elm, for the door's upon her and she walks in. Now, she has disappeared into the Classical building, silence even greater on the campus, for now it's even less coloured – her purse, her gait gone inside. One can imagine her awe at the high ceilings, the general cleanliness of marble. One can imagine her walking to the front desk, asking for a general admission ticket and the museum worker, some graduate student most likely, saying "eight dollars, please, miss," and the woman smiling, producing the ten dollar bill, handing it to the blonde young man in a suit halfly shambled who's got a ruffled copy of Edmund Burke Feldman's *Art as Image and Idea*, used, open to page 236, on the desk in front of him. One can imagine the woman, while waiting for her two dollars in change to be returned, peeking down at the page and seeing Jean Arp's *Star* (1939 – 1960), its five prongs jutting into violent space (in this case, a black background against which the photo of the sculpture was taken). One can imagine even a neophyte like the woman thinking *How stark, how bleak, how did I get into this, but   oh,   you know,   there is something soft about Arp's hollowed-out star . . . something true, something living within the thing;* indeed, Feldman himself of it states "[Arp's star] has gained skin and flesh, with bones implied underneath," so steeped in the organic and the physical is the artist. One can imagine the blond graduate student museum worker catching the attractive thirty-ish woman peering down and thinking she's up to something else, the kind of thing young men dream about all the time and young women never claim to like doing; then, he hands a wrinkled pair of dollars to the woman and wishes her adieu, a "pleasant time in our gallery today." One can imagine the woman thanking the young man, tucking the dollars into her coat pocket, not bothering to snap open her citron purse, then having to decide where to begin—the sculpture wing, the contemporary wing, the others . . . Mara recommended the landscape exhibit, though, so the woman ostensibly will seek it out. One can imagine her helping her seeking by asking a guard: the guard then pointing *there*, to an elevator, then also wishing her *a pleasant day in our museum*, then her smile and her walk toward the elevator, the wait for the light to light the second floor, the opening of the door, the stepping in, the pressing of "3" and the sealing of the box. One can imagine her going up, preparing to see "Landscape in Maine," the exhibit.

If this all happened—if there was a woman with a citron purse strolling into an exhibit named "Landscape in Maine" with the death of her mother on her mind—it happened in 1970. All there "is" now is a program—a perfect-bound, 130-page, black-and-white manual, essentially. Here is where it (the exhibit) (the poem) happened: Bowdoin College, sometime between May 21 and June 28. The exhibit was a traveling one: Colby College and Orono at other times during that spring and summer. Therein the likes of Homer, Marin, Kimball, Kroll, Church, Lane. Thereon canvases Ktaadn, the rocky coast, forests, the Eastports and Kennebunks and Perus and all.

Interpolation of Friend and Objects in a Landscape

My friend is driving through a driving rain—that old cliché,
horizontal rain. How rain can come in horizontally, the sea
may know. It needs to be put to sleep; think of all its pain
when you think of all the sinkings, all the squalls utmost gray
it has endured. For centuries—ages longer than a gold clasp
of forest horizon gripping the sky, as if within the above there's
someone answering. My friend presses on, looking hard at road
dissolving into road, trees stripped from much of the parcel
to her left. There's someone at its end, at the end of road.
There's it sounds like birds, but it's not—beyond cemetery,
beyond the fact its headstones are piled perfectly, like sugar.
For centuries, there's someone answering, voice like saltwater
lapping a piling or two; the someone questioning, voice some-
thing like stones tossed by a child off a dock. All our guesses,
our wonderings—like buoys out there. The revelations—boats
zipping beyond the light blue into the dark. And here we stand
in the light blue, all of us, in the shadow of what is a mariners'
cemetery on the coast. The child will grow up to hate writers,
will grow up like every single tree, in other words. The child
hates words other than shore and Nauticat—a brand of yacht
made in Scandinavia. He spots one!, and quickly forgets by
the time his little palm has thrust another stone in the harbour.
By the time I read this, I remembered the cemetery and the friend
who is my friend driving an oblong state. Sometimes all our minds
are misplaced. What is equilibrium but a shore that keeps getting
lapped, a harbour that keeps lapping. What is madness but the kid
draped in a blue parka, ruining the fluency of the landscape. Blip
and/or blur, this child, his little arm continually flinging rocks
and reaching to the ground and rummaging for the biggest of them
and doing it again: a distraction, like the yellow billboard to our right,
which when seen through a hard rain is like a beacon, a comfort,
but merely advertises an antique shop off the next exit. Look at
this:

perfect state of fields only minorly broken by things like posts, tall weeds—then in the middle of the composition known as Here and Now, This Particular Point on Earth, this billboard. Even the noble rain in streams on the window can't serve as a sufficient re-focuser, re- orientor. Here and now we have a breach, and then and over there on the shore a breach as well: motion of a little boy unsettling Beauty. Enough about the child, enough about the state of rurality. The state of the fields. It hurts to think. The address of the fields, some without upturned roots. My least favourite had a dryad at the heart of it. Hers had some barn. The roof sagged—like most barns seen from a roadway upon which rain berates and berates. Enough. I see road goes on. I see the vision of a far-off boy and beach going. I see the car window and throughout it, no imperfections / and beyond it, a fairly massive swath. I see my friend as a graceful reflection gaining shapes and colours as each mile shutters by. One instant, she smiles and by so doing her teeth line up with the right of a barn's closed door—flying by—slid shut for winter. Slid shut for winter like an animal knowing it's tiny, thence hiding neath a leaf in the midst of a tornado. What was in the antique shop?

Dream

Once upon a time a boy was walking in the forest.
All of a sudden, a goblin jumped out of the bushes.
The goblin brought him to a skeleton-house.
The goblin opened the door and saw his friends in the house.
They love the water, the cleanest lake they'd ever seen.
They hit the road. They remembered going to eat limes.
All of the given kisses good-bye. *I'll just put myself in the water.*
The boy kept dreaming—walking into a foggy lake, those ashore
just watching and eating their citra. The forest hovered in behind
and the house was emptied. All its lamps, on, its door, opened,
its goblin, bored stillborn. No one to scare, nothing ahead of him
in a forest whose occupants chose to quietly watch a boy swim.

Processes (Overheardings)

i look forward to
the midst now of
where we're at right now—
right now—lake,
there   i heard one of
those rumours—fairly
might be three, there's
a line as well, one
of those mathematics
may still be   a fog
search, serving none
a lot of work   fair
share along with piece
of no idea how to.

————————————

more than once. degrees
a lot of common processes.
how one runs   as we
looked yesterday a chance
of flux   whatever next
year useful also's got
some very good way. very
good. very good. a hand.
best best best field
of some help. the future
didn't include any of that.

————————————

generating furthermore also up
on an engine-specific access
if not all spent with him   rest
again   underscore the briefly
having read the risk   want to
properly very much type back
comes from pleased steps to
input   but he needs to be sure.

———————————

one would think should not
hear someone on bodies or
devils. some of us made an
approval as far as an   . is that
flower going dark   we can tell, we
fear lighting anything else.

Asteral (Lyric-like #1)

if you come over i'll give to you what I can

i heard you're in L.A. for the protest and the Post-sit-in
i heard you're in L.A., shirt not buttoned at the top

got a yellow flower patch spiting the horizon line
      got a yellow shirt   whyn't you here to try it on

got some far-off friends' shirts and shoes and socks
      got some far-off friends   their funny baby's very odd

asters in rain   you won't believe how they blow
      asters in rain   you won't believe how they move

got a rock collection and photographs of smoke
      got a road on my mind   whyn't we walk it slow

that bunch of asters on my windowsill   in bloom
      thine bunch of asters callin me   hey pick us soon

asters in rain   you won't believe why they move

You just Keep Going (Tong'Len #1)

you just keep going steady like the sloop on Buzzard's Bay I never did see though I spent decades of leaning over the railings to see it, dropped quarters into the binoculars countless times

you just keep going I stepped out of the shower thinking too much, as I usually do when stepping out of the shower, realizing my life will be perfectly symmetrical on September 16, 2005 (I was born March 16, 1975 = 30 years—> March is 3 months into the year so subtract 3 from 12 for balance's sake = September)

you just keep going so let me keep going with my explanation— so she took this pear and it was shaped like one half of her torso, one side of hip and it was very pretty but I'm too slow

you just keep going while the building keeps sagging, building I dreamt about one October back in grad school, maybe one incorporated into an old poem draft likely never taken too seriously

you just keep going but maybe the neighbor does not, for he wonders how to build a metallic egg. I was once a chauffeur for the stars I was once a little kid-minion for the chicken farmer man

you just keep going and so does night, slow wheels and soda can fizz

you just keep going, all the things your kids say you meant to record but forgot

you just keep going, but the seascape that made such a vast impression on you doesn't give anything to you that's able to be stored in a tiny box under the trundle

you just keep going to the farm atop the hill because you think
maybe someday you'll bump into the adolescent boy and girl
Homer painted in *A Temperance Meeting*

you just keep going and a cryin and a feelin she won't touch you
in the woods like she used to—Kinsman Creek cold and beautiful
falls off the west

you just keep going buoys, you just keep on because the ships all
need you

you just keep going grasses, aimless and up and always if only for
the sun, you just keep on going
never stopping

when I say you just keep going I think everyone out there need
listen
        to the sound of your feet shuffling in beautiful leaves

Man Singing in Vermont (Lyric-like #2)

She's a book in which the pages only let turn in the dark
She's a mobile scuffled with the itch of daybreak in the park

She's the turpentine brought in a pail to see the Van Gogh show
She's the usefulness of skeptics who unearth the lie of snow
and she's out there
she's out there

So I bring her here
for you to see
for you to judge
for us to hear

       that she complies   with the wiles
    of a man done wrong by his own songs.

She outfits all her ice cream trucks with sirens of the law
She outfits all her ice cream laws with sirens of the trucks

She defies a rhyme, defies the cactus, makes the earth her own
She's a playpen with the bars all broke and dumped off at a bar
and she's out there
she's out there

So I bring her here
for you to see
for you to judge
for us to hear

       that she complies   with the wiles
    of a man done wrong by his own songs.

Dissituation (Lyric-like #3)

here a crowd of lonely sited

deeming might impossible

upward looketh children all

see the lining in a cloud

see a life before your eyes

flashing like a stop sign beam

make your life of art no friend

Looking Out a Window (Tong'Len #2)

Woman who died adjacent
to this hallscape of echo'd
limbs, light contours, shape-
shifts of Erie cloudpath—

good woman, you're out
and amidst. You're dangling
and by such thou feed me
and by such bird more divine

by such bird more divine more
birds divine, more seek, I have
to think, a greatest of clouds,
whether whitest or darkest

never known but to the wings
and by that, the bones within
and in those, the compellors
and the motors—all such drive

if be trac'ed back, we would find
you, alone in a rocker, cool sunset
and abandoned. I know too what
going children's like, I know you

in death. I know the window for
it's a friend in trying sunsets, and nary
a week goeth by when you, good
woman, don't call from without it.

Event of Chains

6−5−4,
animal's created

3−2−1,
musicality is proffered

0−1−2,
step up and to the stage

3−4−5,
accept all your rewards

6−7−8,
the children ain't in bed

9−10−11,
satellites are putting

10−9−8,
mannekinite infants

7−6−5,
garden's fringed with bottles

4 − 3 − 2,
your face frisson'd with drap'ry

1 − 0 − 1,
your face render'd in water

2 − 1 − 0,
an object reaches outward

2 − 1 − 0,
all language reaching outward

+ stunt'd by rules of musick

as vines by rules of column

["affix not, yon vine, to wood

                           affix to stone and to brick
and be known for the cover
to brick provided

        in any attempt to affix to
        stone be you render'd to
        mere attempted mem'ry

                some blown + brown dustling
                to be shrivel'd & forgot"]

Dark Tracts

Grandmother Poem

She would not allow him to paint her
She would rather see her face as words
Such a terrible symmetry she knew she'd got
From God or otherwise the zygotia
From hysteria, an otherwise brainwave
which she rode into her gardens
and nightly
and when there she was
(when there she finally was)
only then could she remember
Remember the kiss
How he'd angled his
no, like that
———*no, like this*
Her nose was in his way
In the way of his
having her
She stares the flower down
Purple universe returning
nothing, nothing comes back
Save the anther-like trajectory
known as her clunky, pretty face
Don't paint it, please, son
I can't bear it

Musée Picasso

2005 october 16

in the city palatial with sounds of
all stones, la nu allongé's alone in
recline, skiff of light adash on her
forearm, only light in a maroon room
in which viewers trailed in the rains

in her glass case, la nu allongé's
locked forever in embraces—of walls
readied for show, of viewers' wives
and I was one of the men comparing
her lines to those of mon femme, far

away over some ocean and now a
child's holler on Rue de Citeaux
calling for maman—dissipated
as a million accords, dissolv'ed
as September in an October leaf

    ~

my wife reclines naked as I
and I gorge but she'll be widow
and I, dusted with snowdrops, set
in motion toward becoming forgot
as a scroll locked in a mountain

my wife reclines, her legs pyramid-
edges in angle and shell in timbre
and I, I crouch closely with camera
angling to catch her face ablur, deep,
and her belly, closer and uppropped

there is nothing noble about me, . . .
haven't you seen an ant drawn to sugar
or a brush driven to palette then canvas
and so it goes that subsist I must on
cubes and angles comprising my muse

∽

there is music o la nu allongé paint-
brush tapping palette, treading canvas
slurring l'huile there is music o
in catching one's wife in a moment
music of shutterdrop, of linen and thigh

music of lampswitch of la nuisette
falling music of afterfall of bird
through a window of breeze in a curtain
a cape through which no one may see
the private studio, its tripods or easels

I angle my instrument toward the pretty
and steadily and a breeze may/mayn't billow
the billions of nightshod rooms on earth
the billion paintstrokes for the galleries'
coursing billion tourists silently pacing

∽

did the artists have their way
always or sometimes with
their models depicted always
or sometimes as tender & naive
always legs together just enough

were they selfish artists keeping
from viewers the best, hinting
only hinting the models were real
with real disasters clean and puffy
and manicured and getting ready

and then in a back tea room behind
authority of table or canvas stretcher
ask the girls tender & naive to part
their thighs, cup their spilling breasts,
and if so did they get painted or else

~

where are alternate versions of la nu
allongé, her many cousins the odal-
isques and bathers and reclining riche
tended by washerwomen, fawned over
during luncheons on l'herbe by jerks

sexuality is still an early architecture
the nude a series of obscure cubes
and you can't really smell her reality
la nu allongé can afford to lounge
around her dignity is intact but if

we are ever to express for distant races
what we had once and long ago we
must ask our wives to spill forth that
which makes men want to fuck them
even when four-thousand miles away

Rivers and Oceans

no my boy that is no ocean
that is a mountain's extremely feeble attempt to become a woman

yes your mother is a woman
she is a coeur de mal i will string it from an airplane skid the
water's surfeit

ocean water holds no truths no
only poets talk that way it holds millions of dead sailors dead
swordfish

ocean water is a lie your mother
reclined against me once on a beach now she avoids people though
she's a nurse

she likes to help people or so
she thinks she does no one knows themselves we are developing
processes

some try to actualize talk of
knowledge and experience as being like oceans but oceans have
shores they end

knowledge and experience limited are
not so essentially you will row from today with what i've told you

keep on rowing until you run out of
steam someone else will come along and steer the ship a river ship

life moves in a line an ocean is circle
dotted with whitecaps thousands of bluescrapers below the
airplane belly

oceans are contained rivers aren't
even dams crack and explode man is a stupid beast he can't hold
thought back

though he tries by building dams putting
pens to paper but there is always much more beyond the struc-
ture
the words

it is insufficient yes you are right
you are precocious little humming son now seven you have
devastated me

you stared at me two minutes after
the nurse took you from your mother you knew me you really did
i saw it

river between your eyes and my eyes
the first stare the first awareness you snared me in your ocean i
am blocked

i shall float here always my time is gone
now is your time take the ship head upriver quickly while you
can quickly

go on and on forever, never stop for her
stop when you feel sated and i'll await you somehow here way
over here

in what will be a vast distance
my settling to the bottom of ocean your triumphant river ride
toward the sun

So You Want to Be a Sailor

but you haven't the thumbs for it
they fall off in slight breeze
you haven't the knowledge though
you've the knowledge of stars
you can't handle home as it sinks
in some far-fogged thinness broken
by birdcall's spray of seablight,
pilings battend all Novembre and you
you haven't a need for Novembre
and to navigate without love spring
and autumn causes you something
likely commonly known as pain, like
some batterd rock feeleth when with
seastroke is smote, when with dark
is smote   you can't imagine nightfall
on a shore alone as a sea stone—you
think life is rickety enough on land
why do you feel this way, one means,
why do you wish to sail my friend
into the recessing sunlight, spilling
off one's eyes into a winter tomorrow
known as the cold cave of space, you
are no kin to the waters to the vapours
to the map and depth chart, why death
chart be damned, you would have it
to drive right into a shallows to call
the great bluff and to make her back
home wonder where you were forever
but you need to know my friend you do
they do not build widows' watches nomore
and wives haven't time to pace them nohow

Bells from the Courtyard

There were no bells from the courtyard last night
Get on with life as you normally would

Get on with your life as you normally would
Go about your daily routine be normal

There are usually bells from the courtyard at night
Go about your daily routine be normal

No one has wed in the courtyard for months
The courtyard's a place where couples make vows

To live and to formulate daily routines, nothing
Has happened so go on with life and be normal

There are dying bouquets stacked in the corner
The courtyard smells like dying flowers go on

And keep decaying decay even beyond decay
Go on with your normal routine and daily go on

The brides don't whisper of the courtyard's majesty
Don't you know the girlfriends used to whisper

Get on with your life as you normally would
No one has wed in the courtyard for months

Go on with your normal routine and daily go on
Go on with your normal routine and daily go on

The bell was removed from the courtyard last night
Removed by six strong men in gabardines and hats

The bell has been taken seven towns over it was
Melted in a foundry go on with your life go on

There are usually bells from the courtyard at night
I said the bell was taken seven towns over it was

The courtyard is closed there are sentries in front
Go on with your normal routine and daily go on

It is alright go on with your daily routine and go on
The bell was melted in a foundry go on with your life

There are sentries in front of the courtyard there are
They wield rifles bright bronze shells litter the ground

Get on with your life as you normally would
The bell was converted in a foundry go on son go on

There are more and more bright shells on the ground daily
Go on with your normal routine and daily go on

There are more and more bright shells on the ground daily
I can't see through the courtyard gate too many sentries

Go on with your normal routine and daily go on
No one has wed in the courtyard for months

Yes but I wonder what is going on in the courtyard
They wield rifles bright bronze shells litter the ground

There are dying bouquets stacked outside the gate daily
More and more dying bouquets stacked outside the gate

Go on with your normal routine and daily go on
Go on with your normal routine and daily go on

Go on with your normal routine and daily go on
No one has died in the courtyard for hours

Go Toward the Window

no substantial cloud, a wispy mackerel
one of trillions way up there out of place
out of its rightful place i will pull it as

i pull words from the array of a field in
every direction out the window spilling
every artist i've loved laboring in it on its

sill rests a queketti   help me   walk toward it so
i may study your motion or milky expression
and forlorn hour of the searcher the looking

Where Has the Pastoral Gone?

no boys recline together on the grass
no watermelon slices between them passed
no barn yard in the background no field
no leaning on the fence watching father
weaning the calf, no climbing the second rung
as the young girl in a dress whispers

as the night air gone
forever as it is
so far off

as the millions of miles
of seashores so far off
hear the ocean speak

story of dissipation,
disappearance

no more fire-ochres and rust-browns
no hand-hewn wood and sifted wheats
no glint in the calf's eye of his mother
as he is tethered and pulled, weaned
no after-school leisure with a book
with a friend and his far-off gaze

at the night air going
off someplace and
that place is sad

as the millions of miles
between that sad place
and himself add up

muchly white
between worlds

~

no spiders write today
nor do the painters paint

many poets are going unnoticed
no crime there

many shores are being discovered
by lovers

many oceans are spewing up stones
erodedly chalky like god

many books get their yellow tinge
from the dying sun of July

or November wherein a breeze
is sad like an empty workshop

or rabbit coop—deserted because
one's grandfather slips into time

many artists' works linger abrain
the working poet

many texts and songs and photos
too linger there

and despite all the terrains real
and fictive

and motivated by same and
by admiration for those works

they re-appear in, as the words,
ideas of the working poet

working hard to feel, to honour
not to imitate yet

yet the whole time he is somehow not
real, therefore not happy

he is happy to be free to be well-fed
but he knows no man

to be authentic he knows all men
to be condemned

he knows something in the colours
of the canvases he saw when young

in a library book he read on the floor
as his mother perused periodicals

his six-year-old moptop deep and black
nothing like the ragged gray

he can see the boy eyeing the spines
making sure his wasn't on loan

and he can see the boy anxiously open
to the worlds of others

and he can see the boy frightened
at those worlds

and drawn into wanting to see
or feel what those artists or

their subjects or their landscapes
felt—then, later, the boy grew

and went away from painting
and got mixed up in words for

many years, then mountains, then
love, then it came to the point

when he had become an aggregate
of not all he'd ever done or seen

but of all that others had fed him,
bestowed upon him

and like a barn door opens far away
in a distant memory, hundreds of

years old, like that door slowly opens
to reveal bales—the working poet

slowly writes a tract that slowly reveals
as it goes along varied in form

varied in concern and stance
varied in vernacular

that slowly reveals that
which from outside has been gifted

that slowly reveals the theft that
has occurred over three decades

theft of the author disappearance and
dissipation of the author the

working poet become a carriage for
the continuity of others' ideas

but is this problematic it could be
commonplace

all we know is the bales are there
and mellowing

the onset of winter will make them
useless

until they are discovered in their
frozen state by a new figure

maybe a boy who climbs upon them
with vigour

and enjoys their texture, heft,
core of ice

that will strike him at that one right moment
and linger in him always

recognition of something beyond all
he can see or touch

recognition of something churning
his fist-sized stomach

is it "fear" or is he feeling "pleasure" at
his discovery

and in relating this discovery to others
at a later time

will he walk unguided through a field or
will he walk as our working poet,

who spills his intoxication with the ideas of
other artists onto his tract

and hell will the field even be there given
our state of progress

it may all be moot for perhaps on the way's
that which will make obsolete

expression and discovery I mean look
look at what has already occurred

no boys recline together on the grass
no watermelon slices between them passed

no barn yard in the background no field
no leaning on the fence watching father

no climbing the second rung
as the young girl whispers

of the night air gone
forever it is so

far off as
the millions of miles

of seashores so far off
hear the ocean speak

Ekphratic Particulates

i.	ii.	iii.	iv.
every	a	unless	as
thing	thing	it	opposed
was	tangible	be	to
once	was	of	the
some	once	the	world
thing	a	natural	of
else.	notion,	world	ideas.

∾

i.	ii.	iii.	iv.
a	so	and	. . . uh,
poet	he	there	'sitting'
wants	goes	he	on
to	to	sees	the
write—	the	paintings	ground,
so	local	hanging	then
it	art	or	he
goes.	museum	sculptures	writes.

∾

i.	ii.	iii.	iv.
a	so	to	with
poet	he	what	which
wants	goes	he	he
to	to	knows	is
write—	his	—ideas	familiar,
so	memory	or	and
it	so	things	adopts
always	he	he	their
goes.	goes	admires,	spirit.

~

i.	ii.	iii.	iv.
content	the	(actual	and
gotten	poet	galleries	will
now	may	of	ultimately
the	look	art,	find
poet	inside	otherwise	that
needs	his	books,	particular
form—	many	journals,	form
so	repositories	songs,	befitting
it	for	buildings,	his
goes.	insight	landscapes)	content.

~

i	*ii.*	*iii.*	*iv.*
the	is	but	is
poet	there,	what	this
finishes	borne	troubles	'mine,'
writing	of	the	or
and	many	poet	an
what	places	is,	extension
is	and	"where'm	of
there	influences—	'i'?	_____?"

∾

i.	*ii.*	*iii.*	*iv.*
"and	of	did	would
if	another,	'i'	'i'
it	where	go	look
is	am	?	like
an	'i'	and	any-
extension	where	what	way?"

∾

i.	ii.	iii.	iv.
"have	i	into	to
'i'	has	an	an
been	dis-	other	other
thieved?	solved	in	another"

≈

i.	ii.	iii.	iv.
"then	beach,	line?	are
whose	shore-	whose	they?"

≈

i.	ii	iii.	iv.
"is	creating	to	befear?"

Rocky Coast, Maine, March 1975

The author was born during this month,
during this year, not far from this beach—

that is what calm looks like. That it is warm
on this earth at any time of year, ever, enrages

so many. They will not fly balloons because
the updraft of dusty sunlight from a forest floor

interferes with the iodes of their dresses, ballast-
ed by the greens and burgundies of deep woods

made out of the sprinklings of a celestial wreck.
The author saw the bay this morning, deciding

to write about water. In a curtain's dumb yellow
he saw what he fancied to be an allusion—

the arrival of Ur-Orpheus—and then decided
he didn't write about things like that. Things

like breakers and fogbanks intrigued him, so
he wrote about breakers and fogbanks and

he wrote in actuality about Homer's breakers,
the ones Homer'd seen in 1898 at Prout's Neck,

the fogbanks Homer'd seen shrouding vessels off
the coast of Tynemouth, England. The ones he

himself had seen lacked all drama and into them
no drama could be built. It is hard to dramatize

water and shorelines when neon signs behind you
seek to murder you with commerce. Hard to be

authentic when the source of is is no longer. Yes
friends hard to convince anyone of any vision for

any length of time for the visions are all here!,
everything of Ulro all gone Vegas and Manhattan.

The writer's apologia is to look at the waste of
the progressive present and kill it through renewal

of the art of the past when death was as major
as a fallen log high on an Adirondack dome —[1]

⁓

Soon, your favourite tidal marsh will make its procession from
out the fogbanks. Its band of ochre will loll on the horizon, and
you'll nestle in the bilge in your parka. The vessel will reeve
through the block of dense air, dense grey, don't you fear. I won't
soon forget the red clay of Cape Tormentine, how your eyes leapt
at it—I won't forget those little marlin spikes, easing the heft of
the pull of my fears. We're off-soundings but will track southwest,
toward any lighthouse that'll help. It's alright, babe, we're going
back to harbour after the trajectory of long travel.

---

[1] *isn't death just so prehistoric nowadays? Anyone*
   have any good jokes to tell? Anyone? Yes, you! . . .

Water Colour

After all the leaves relinquish like dropt chaplets
After their hues are determined to be reparative
After sunset's nephelinia coats all the seaboard
After the mynyms of a trolley's wheels pass away
After silence after all these proceedings becoming
Dark heavy grosgrain of the distant farm fields
Dark three-part breath of the evening daunen
Dark lunettes of horizon-lit prows near a lighthouse
Dark sea in its perpetual churn Dark hum of air
Dark universe in perpetual turn Dark mind adrift
Then I will turn to turn in for the night as usual
Then I will drift home with both hands apocket
Then I will listen to the nearby authentic water
Then I will, full and content as the empty harbour

Thief of Shells

He takes them for they are "wondrous,"
as he tells his friends over drinks.

He goes drawn to the shore all the time,
the others off to their belfries.

When he crosses the golden streets,
he likes to chart the birds' palavering

coming from an Atlantic shrub. Atop
a sidewalk bench (he need stand on it

for she cannot see over the seawall)
he measures today's flutter of flags

against the paraphs of yesterday. He
is enamoured of wash, of its wind.

He has a favourite tidal pool—some-
one else has his own, maybe same.

At any rate, he will look for the shells
in and around the pool, where boulders

pock like swage blocks. Each white-
ness is a revelation—little tracts,

little plots, thousands of them, dust-
dropped on three miles of shoreline.

He smiles at the sight. He wants all
day to pick up each and every one,

knowing full well this to be possible
because life, spent right, is limitless.

He smiles and begins by stooping
for the common oyster at his feet.

He will traverse the century of beach
until the inevitable rain of dusk

brings the possibility-drowning tide,
his disappointed, fog-dark walk home.

~

'Thief' is a strong word. He does homage,
not theft. And, at any rate, he would say

the shells would want him to do it, to bring
them to his mantel. There, on snowy days

for the next decades until he's gone, their
curves and slight shallow bellies and ivory

colours will provoke him. He will look down
his array, hundreds of gently uneven silences,

or even naiads, since they once rested some-
where much more pastoral, a place they were

never even perceived of as separate realities
until someone like him took the care to see,

to notice. Yes, he has his favourites, going
up to them time and again, as when a friend

coughs. Or when autumn erases the once-hearty
colors of his herbs until obituarial black seeps

in, and they huddle against the dun New England
of the soil in submission to season, to volcanical

unholy skies. Or when he is merely sad for reasons
that any of us become sad. He cites his favourite

shells daily; they hang in his mind as footnotes
when appropriate—a new wrought-iron lamp

adorned with garlands makes him think *astarte*,
the joy of his wedding day so very far removed

reminds him of the shape of the lightning whelk,
the pink cockle of a ribbon in his daughter's hair

as they walked across a wide, warm field, the smile
they shared out there beneath the vast, utter sky of

possibility, all friends were the banks of cirrus and
the darting cinnamon veeries. Now, his cottage is

cold. He pulls on his sweater, glancing out at gray
with no real way of explaining his sadnesses . . .

∾

He keeps on collecting, keeps cluttering
her mantel. He keeps loving all he has

to love. He meets with friends but it's all
just bittersweet. At night, his array moves

him to speak, so he does, to the silent
room. Wall calendar, miniature lighthouse,

multimodal quilt. Creaking earth, winnow
of autumnal beach breeze. He goes on,

speaking until he nods off. He will comb
his hair brusquely come morning, then read

his shells. Sometimes their reds and ivories
will move him to walk to the shore, some-

times not. In his happier moments, he's
got a notion that these shells stole him,

piece-by-piece, one shell by one shell, in
the end removing him from the world,

from the landscape. He smiles, feeling
he's been filled with thousands of joys.

He then, without fail, will sip gently a beer
and rock the swing, slowly, all arbours pay-

ing to him their attention, almost; the branch
lovingly above his head, his eyes wistful; and

see each shell as a marker on a map of his
life, life not as empty of life as would seem.

Notes

Continae: the Contina is a camera made by Zeiss. In honour of its excellent and dignified name, "continae," then, are any kinds of recordings (visual and/or aural in nature).

Dream: the first four lines are by Samuel Paquin.

The Exhibit: there is an actual exhibition guidebook. There is no given date or place of publication, but it is titled Landscape in Maine 1820-1970 and contains a foreword and introduction written by James M. Carpenter. The exhibit traveled to Colby and Bowdoin colleges, and the University of Maine-Orono, in 1970.

Grandmother Poem is not about my grandmother, whose face is anything but asymmetrical or clunky, but more like the poem's garden, full of possibility and generosity and many extraordinary seasons.

Printed in the United States
71622LV00001B/168